A RIPPLE

A Ripple

Poems by
Mary Sloan

FLOATING ISLAND PUBLICATIONS
POINT REYES STATION
1986

Cover painting by James Sloan

Published by:

Floating Island Publications
P.O. Box 516
Point Reyes Station, California 94956

Designed and produced by Michael Sykes at Archetype West,
Point Reyes Station, California.

Printed and bound by Thomson-Shore, Inc., Dexter, Michigan.

*With special thanks to Rolly Kent, Susan North, Michael Cuddihy,
Tony Hoagland, Evelyn Elster, Betty Creath and Ed Garrett.*

*To my children
and their children*

CONTENTS

9 / Mystery in the Fog

10 / Blue Heron

11 / Alone

12 / Weed of the Sea

13 / Seven-Year-Old Cake Bake

15 / The Death of a Brother

17 / Fishing

18 / Pepper Tree Swing

20 / Conception, 1904

22 / Secrets

23 / Song of the Torrey Pines

24 / Not Yet

25 / Hands

26 / Search

29 / Something of El Greco

30 / Remembering Roadside Rendezvous with Michael

32 / The Snowflake and the Laurel Leaf

33 / Cavu

34 / The Great Blue Whale

37 / A Quiet Place

38 / Requiem

39 / To Be Continued

MYSTERY IN THE FOG

Fog so thick
    The lovers
        Almost invisible

Without sound
    Only water
        Lapping

No sun nor sky
    Darkness
        Tide coming in

The suitor
    Slipped away
        Alone

Water at her feet
    Higher, higher
        Could not move

Quietly he appears
    Lifts her deeper
        Into foggy cove

No words
    Two foggy bodies
        Clinging

BLUE HERON

Black clouds kept descending
    Mysterious and threatening
No light, no light at all

Impenetrable forces
    Moving directionless
Only the silence heard

Then something unusual
    Happened – a rare blue bird
Promenaded by the pond

Where had this magnificent
    Creature come from?
Had he lost his flock in the clouds?

His lovely body
    With plumes drooping
He needed his mate

Alone and forlorn
    Across the pond he
Paddled – searching, seeking

This is a somber day
    Gentle creature
Let me share your loneliness

When the darkness lifts
    We will find our loved ones
Among the white clouds

ALONE

A dark storm thunders
    Over the hills and down to the lake
Watching from the shore it seems
    A girl in white rises effortlessly
She floats or glides in the breeze
    Right into the water

Is she a vision in all that greyness?
    The mist is becoming thicker but
I can still see her
    Wavering at the water's edge
What will become of her in the deepening
    Greyness? Flashes of lightning
Reveal the boat moving toward her

WEED OF THE SEA

For centuries
    Oriental toilers
Mightily raked the shores
    For purple seaweed
Their staff of life

This Chondrus Crispus rides
    The waves with surfers in Hawaii
Accompanies the dhows off Diego Garcia
    Shadows the sampans near Tsingtao

In Kamakura the seaweed
    Wave riding
Pays homage to
    Great Buddha

Remember the weed of the sea
    Food, fuel and vitality
Long an intimate acquaintance
    Japanese, Chinese, Malaysian,
Philippino

Down a hill in San Francisco
    To the St. Francis
Where guests gather
    From over the globe

Waiters scurry with laden trays
    First course – SUSHI
Served on an antique
    Imari platter

Many blocks down the same street
    An old Oriental toiler squats
In the shade of an empty warehouse
    Eating from a brown bag
A SPAM sandwich

SEVEN-YEAR-OLD CAKE BAKE

I had already gone to school
knew how to read and write
was told all about sex
by an older school girl
I knew about my father's
night visits to my mother's bed
It was a custom to take lunch
to the men working in the fields
and because
some visitors had consumed
all the coffee cake
my mother suggested I
bake a cake
To me it was like being
invited to the Pillsbury Bakeoff
my mother was known for her
prize triumphs in baking but
it was one thing I had not attempted
I was ecstatic
we looked through the "White House"
cookbook—my mother's baking bible

As a starter a one egg vanilla
was suggested
I was made to follow directions
explicitly—greasing the pan,
dusting it with flour,
beating the egg, measuring the
dry ingredients—beating and
beating
Each new step a thrill
then finally into the oven
waiting   anxious   nervous
finally the aroma
my nostrils dilated
someone fetched a broomstraw
to test for doneness

Mother, sister and I set
out for a rather long walk
for the lunch in the fields
lemonade and cake carefully toted
I cherished the smell of that
warm cake every step of the way
Father and brothers were duly
appreciative
but my pride needed no bolstering
I had created something with
my hands — I knew it was good
as I gazed dreamily at
my father and brothers
killing a rattlesnake
just a few yards away

THE DEATH OF A BROTHER

I'll always remember
    My baby brother
Lying on a soft silk pillow
    In a little box
And the long line of carriages
    Driving down the lane to
The big road.

Papa gave him the medicine
    He screamed and all his body
Moved everywhere—Mama quickly
    Put him in a tub of warm water
The crying stopped, he didn't move
    Mama screamed, "He's dead"
Papa groaned, "He can't be, he can't"
    Mama wrapped the baby in a blanket
Held him close as she sat in the rocker
    Tears running down her face
Shaking all over.

Papa cried out, "That doctor was drunk,
    I shouldn't have given him the
Medicine, the druggist told me not to
    Oh God, what have I done, I killed
My own baby"
    I began to cry and clutch Mother's
Apron—"Mama, what is dead?"   I sobbed
    Mama stopped crying and put the baby
In his crib and covered him with a blanket.

Mama took me in her arms, "He's
    With the angels in heaven," then to
Papa, "Stop blaming yourself, you did
    What you had to. Come now, we must
Get the children to bed, then
    Telephone the family."

There was no more crying, I felt better
    The other children and I
Moved up the stairs – but before
    I fell asleep I wondered
Where's heaven?

Next morning the house was full of people
    Hugging and kissing us – tearful Mama
Was being loved by her sisters – Papa
    Looked mad trying to explain the terrible
Doctor and what the druggist said

In the garden we cut flowers
    And pinned them on the cloth that
Hung from the table under the
    Little white box.

My brother's smile so quiet and pretty
    I saw those little hands
That grabbed my curls and pulled
    When I played piggy with his toes
He squealed and laughed
    Why was he an angel now?

My baby brother, even though I was
    Only three – the white box
With the silk pillow
    The long line of carriages
The little cousin standing beside me
    Asking, "Where are they taking him?"
And me answering, "To heaven."

FISHING

On a lazy Sunday afternoon
    On an old log under a big oak tree
We put out our hooks, sometimes caught a minnow or two
    It was so peaceful and if we didn't
Get a nibble we threw stones
    Everyone tries to make a ripple on the stream —
Do you remember, meandering in the stream
    Under sleepy old oaks

PEPPER TREE SWING

The monstrous monsoon
   Moved in quickly
Great gray and black clouds
   Swooped recklessly
Lightning and thunder
   Clashed and roared

The storm hit
   I ran to my adobe
Shelter – leaving behind
   My dangling swing
Strung on a sturdy branch
   Of my favorite Pepper Tree

Wind gathered
   Tremendous momentum
Like a feather that
   Giant pepper tree was
Picked up and dropped
   Over the crushed wall
Jagged roots torn
   From the earth
Bruised, writhing

Left stunned memories
   From dollhood
To high-heel days
   And boys
How the birds sang from the
   Willowy branches
Such soft melodies
   Lazy moon-cast shadows
Darted on the walls
   A very private retreat

To swing up and up
    In joy or disappointment
Dreams of a million adventures
    Skiing down snowy mountains
Skating on silvery lakes
    Sometimes praying or singing
Enchanted and longing
    For some great happening
Swinging to the stars, to the moon
    And beyond
The tree that knew and held
    All my dreams

No more — no more
    I trundle my dreams back
To some deep mind recess
    My tears, like the rain, falling
A hatchet hacks those throbbing
    Roots into splinters
A saw screeches and grinds
    The trunks and branches
Into a pile of nothing
    A tractor pushes my matted swing
Down into the deep hole
    Will all my secrets
Crumble with it

All that is left — a new lonely
    Mound of earth
Friends, tread softly
    My girlhood lies buried here

CONCEPTION, 1904

The flame through the
isinglass window of
the old stove flickered
as March winds
hissed down the chimney

Mother and Father shivered
decided to forego the hot
mug of cider – instead they
chose the downy warmth of
the great feather bed

Father was very aware of
the shyness of his wife
they bounced and played
sometimes touching – then
turning away, lost in folds
of feathers

Soon cozy and warm – oblivious
to the vicious storm raging
Father slipped out of his
night shirt and coaxed Mother
to do likewise

First demurring – he began
helping her undo the buttons
both unclad now – bodies
close together – he kissed
her gently on the lips

Whispering into her ear sweet
endearments, his lips moved
down her throat, huddling and
cuddling, his hand caressed
her warm body

His lips on enlarged nipples
of her arched breasts yearning
for more. Her excitement conquered
her shyness as he moved down to
her smooth little belly

Clutching her rounded buttocks
he slipped
quietly into her quivering
body – sensuous motion, rising
and falling – the feather cover
undulating

Both bodies enfolded
engulfing passion intensifying
in a spontaneous moment
a great thrust – a gasp –
followed by delightful squeals
gurgles of pure joy

Undulating covers subside as
does the breathing of the lovers
languidly relishing their
fulfillment

SECRETS

What came between us
      Was always in darkness
So easy, so often
      No one ever knew

SONG OF THE TORREY PINES

We gathered pine cones
And built tiny shrines
In a bed of soft needles
From the dark Torrey Pines

My life ruined by memories
And plagued with "what ifs"
I remember the sunset
How waves dashed the cliff

Or was it the sound
Of my pounding heart
As the pines witnessed
Pledges that we'd never part

You sailed far away
I'm alone with the pines
Our soft bed of needles
And pine cone shrines

I come here often
Lie in our soft bed
To hear the squirrels
Quarreling overhead

In the mothering shadows
Of the soft forest floor
I hear your love words
And believe them once more

NOT YET

A fragile flower
    Not yet a blossom
Petals falling

A voice that
    Wells up
But never becomes
    A song

A hand-guided brush
    Lines of painting
Not yet visible

A naked protozoa
    Shifting in the sea
Too deep for reaching

A sonnet written
    Its depths
Not yet perceiving

A needle threads
    Garment torn that
Should not need mending

A runaway heart
    Lost in
Shadowed meetings

Now a crossroad
    Right or wrong
Not yet knowing

HANDS

These weary hands
Rough to touch
Broken nails
Arthritic

Wrinkled and stained
Better gloved
Too swollen for rings
But strong, strong enough

These are the hands that
Wiped my tears
Blew my nose
Scratched my itches

Painted rainbows
Penned poems
Wrote letters of love or
Bereavement

Spanked my babies
Then held them tenderly
Shook outstretched hands
Glad or greedy

Picked up the pieces
Of empty dreams
Turned the faucet for water
Stirred cake and kneaded bread

Lifted little ones
Stroked the old in kindness
Slapped the sands of time
Then joined together in prayer

SEARCH

I

Up a barren highland to a great
   Old house, ridged by spruce
And maple – entered drafty
   Manor listened to ferocious
Winds hiss through the leaves
   And into every nook
A peat fire smoldered in crumbling
   Stone fireplace

Inga, a seer of sorts, crouched to the
   Right of the fire, poked the
Ashes into bright clusters of sparks

On a low table, a down-tufted cozy
   Warmed the tea pot and delicate
Teacups stood at attention
   Family members gathered
Inga, with a slow cackle, murmured
   Her intention of telling
Our fortunes from the tea leaves

The house moaned in the wind
   Candles flickered as we sipped
Tea in eerie silence
   On my left, Kirsten's cup passed
To Inga whose long transparent
   Fingered hands fondled the
Porcelain, twisting it slowly until
   The leaves fell in a proper pattern

Kirsten's eyes saddened with tears when
    Inga groaned
"Prepare yourself – a terrible disaster
    Will overtake you"
But Sonya danced and sang as the seer drawled
    "You'll be on the stage,
You will be a star"

A young lad, Jon, remained seemingly
    Unmoved when told
"You'll be marching off to war"
    For me, the last, Inga seemed to know
"You must travel much farther, go many places
    But somewhere in the highest mountains you
Will find your answers, the winds will tell you"

II

New strangers helped me on the way to
    Tibet – up steep mountain sides, with
Only a pause to turn the prayer wheel
    Then down deep canyons and ever, and ever
And ever, up and down again, always remembering
    To turn the prayer wheel at each new
Dizzying height

The quiet silence, I listen for sounds
    But all I hear is the breeze tinkling
Wind bells, signalling from monastery to
    Monastery, where the speechless monks
Are pacing, engrossed in prayer

I look out to ever higher mountains
     Huddled in snow caps, or cuddled in snowy blankets
Beauty and endless grandeur, in a world away
     From the world, peace and understanding flow
Through me and in that thin bitter cold air, I
     Become warm inside and sink on the monastery
Steps to rest – a small bird warbles his evensong
     A light wind softly tousles my hair and I
Drift into a dreamy sleep

Am I dreaming now?
     Did a covey of monks, bird-like, raise me
Up and down the great mountain sides
     Effortlessly, till at the bottom
Did they put me on a tram,
     Point the way home and smile?

They helped
     The search is never over, but
Each journey brings answers
     As new questions are raised

SOMETHING OF EL GRECO

El Greco's Saint Bartholomew
   Enfolded in a great golden cloak
Aquiline nose veering off sharply
   One hand sword upheld
The other chained to a small devil
   Inscription: "Never mind the
Devils outside — just get rid of
   The ones inside you"

REMEMBERING ROADSIDE
RENDEZVOUS WITH MICHAEL

Panting pavement
   Cooled by tall
Eucalpytus' lazy leaves
   Shadowing across
Fields to horseshoe
   Ridge of pines
Imagining still farther
   Ocean waves lapping
Scorching sand

Michael in wheelchair
   Companion's flattened
Body resting in roadway
   I pause to chat
But summer's intense
   Searing heat
Leaves minds engulfed
   In private silence
More remote than stars

Finally I mention
   That my fragmented
Thoughts seem not to
   Conform to rigors
Of grammar –
   Dashes suit
My pattern better

M's head bowed for
   Breath, then with
Penetrating blue eyes
   Peering over glasses

His slightly smiling
   Lips attest to his
Preference for the colon:
   Bowing head again for air
Eyes twinkling, wide grin —
   "It's the anticipation
Of what comes after"

We agreed our
   Metaphors are not
Always understood
   Stillness again
Away from noisy
   Tormenting world
We listen to the
   Inaudible

THE SNOWFLAKE AND THE LAUREL LEAF

A snowflake glimmered and lingered
    On a tiny laurel leaf
Afraid of melting under the sun's
    Bright sheath
The leaf enfolded the icy snow
    And into his frail thin veins
The moisture flowed

They became one and sustained each other
    The laurel tree grew like a stalwart mother
And the little leaf in the sunny breeze
    Danced there happily,
Remembering the snowflake on a tiny
    Leaf of the laurel tree

CAVU

Ascending to the tune of
    Fire-hearted jet engines
As they combine elements
    Of earth and air
Among wandering tides
    From stratus to cumulus on
Through cirrus we climb –
    A great blue dome above –
Heaven's wilderness

Below drifting clouds linger
    On horizon's rim
The last blush of Day
    Floating on masses
Of visible vapor
    The magenta streak of
Her pulsing pudendum
    Trembling, humming
As majestic black Night
    Descends to enfold her
In mystery, bliss and darkness

Only the stars look on
    And become lights
As we float down
    Gravity reclaiming us

THE GREAT BLUE WHALE

Swim out into life's
    Great adventure
All you terra firma beings
    Release your minds
Beyond static day visions

Contemplate seventy million
    Years ago with evolving
Sea creatures on a single
    Land Continent

From swimmers to
    Four-legged animals
Attaining enormous stature
    The whale competing
With the Dinosaurs

Go forward
    Five million years when
The great whale, weary
    With land-living
Longs for freedom

The ears bend inwards, the
    Forearms fold into great fins
The tail a giant fan
    Seventy-five feet across
One hundred fifty graceful tons

In the icy floes of Antarctica
    We find Daco
Diving and swimming happily
    With fellow companion, Manto
It is mating time and
    Great anticipation finds

Them migrating to a warmer clime
    Leaving the turbulent
Wilderness of the floes behind

Daco begins his mating song
    His voice, like an Aeolian Harp,
Magical and eerie in sound
    Carried on wind currents to
His far-away mate, off the coast
    Of Paraparamuamua
In the lee of an island,
    A sand-strewn cavern –
"Hi-lo lea – si si san na mo mano so no la"

A joyous reunion
    Flapping and diving, free abandonment
Their mirth as uncontrolled as the
    Plankton they feed on
They splash and play
    Two long years since their last mating

A soft moon stirs an
    Elemental longing
Games of touch, fins patting
    Fins, bodies curving in
Shimmering circles waltz-like
    Round and round,
Circling in, circling out

Manto moves beneath Cea
    Gently nudges and raises
Her massive body upward
    While gleaming body of Daco
Circles closer closer

Manto deftly turns her over
    Daco delicately strokes
Her mammae with his fin
    Causing a frenzy of desire
Softly chants his love song
    "Hi-lo lea – si si san
Na mo mano so no la"

In fast tempo, Manto brings
    Ceo to the surface
Daco with a quick swirl
    Moves to enfold her
In ecstasy and delight down
    They plunge into the depths
Of their beings, uniting
    In rhythm with the waves

Their bodies thrill
    To the sensuous pressures
The last great thrust
    Convulsive quiver and throb
Overwhelming moment
    Sobs of fulfillment
They float through the night
    In their own wonderment

Swim back into life's
    Great adventure
All you terra firma beings
    Release your minds
Beyond static day visions
    Not eighty yesteryears
Nor a million billion
    A vast chain link fence of
Cells unites the whole
    Living world

Listen to the Song of the Whale

A QUIET PLACE

From a lifetime of up and down
    Long roads of travel
Only the serene quiet of an abbey
    Brought me comfort and peace

Now when I look up the long road
    My faltering steps failing with
So much still to be accomplished
    Retirement to the abbey is what I need

Two moments stand out vividly

Once as a child, I experienced a
    Great feeling of fulfillment
That did not relate to anyone
    Around me

Once alone, visiting a Shinto Shrine
    High in the mountains
I felt a Presence all around
    Great peace within

REQUIEM

At twilight I seek
Surcease of body woes
Rest in meadow's grass
In an old oak's shadow

In the stillness I
Abandon earth in eternal sleep
How wonderful at last to realize
The true meaning of *Requiescat in pace*

Loved ones stand by
Grieving and weeping
Dry your tears, dear ones
There is no need to cry

At twilight look to the
Long shadow of the oak tree
In the cool breeze
Where tall grass ripples

I am not gone
My presence is among you
Listen and understand
The night stillness

TO BE CONTINUED

Down the hill from the old farm house
    To a stream where ferns and violets grew
To a steamboat ride on the Mississippi
    Married, driving Route Five between
Dubuque and Chicago or through the farmlands
    In Wisconsin or on to the Shenandoah Valley
Watching the sunsets off Casco Bay down
    To the fall leaves dropping in upstate New York
Then sailing in the Gulf of Mexico, soft and
    Tropical – the long, long train ride
From New York to California and again the
    Much longer ride across the Pacific
By way of the cold, forlorn Aleutians
    To the heat of Okinawa, finally to the
Never-ending beauty of Japan – architecture,
    Landscape, mountains and sea – then the
Romance of the Hawaiian Islands to
    Visiting with old friends from World War II
Tours in the country around Sidney and New Zealand
    Flanked by glaciers, mountains and oceans
On every side
    Later in the States with five grandchildren we
Drove from Chicago to Niagara Falls, through
    Canada, everyone feasting on corn on the cob
Widowed, I traveled alone to
    Europe, Scotland a gloaming and hillside
Reverie, the crushed-togetherness of England,
    The lights of Paris and the wonders of
The Versailles Palace, thoughts about the ghosts
    Of Marie Antoinette and Napoleon
How the pride of the conquerors, worm-eaten
    In their own dust no matter what their grand
Rank and conquests – four coffins and a golden
    Dome over Napoleon may not atone for his
Days of exile
    My journey to be continued –

DESIGNED AND PRODUCED IN THE SUMMER OF 1986 BY MICHAEL SYKES
AT ARCHETYPE WEST IN POINT REYES STATION, CALIFORNIA.
PRINTED AND BOUND IN AN EDITION OF 500 COPIES
BY THOMSON-SHORE, INC., DEXTER, MICHIGAN.
THE TYPE FACE IS CASLON 540
AND WAS SET ON AN EDITWRITER 7500.
THE COVER PAINTING IS BY JAMES SLOAN.

Other Titles from Floating Island Publications

Peter Wild, *Barn Fires*
    32 pp, perfectbound, $3.00
Frank Graziano, *Desemboque*
    48 pp, perfectbound, $4.00
Christine Zawadiwsky, *Sleeping With The Enemy*
    32 pp, perfectbound, $4.00
Jeffery Beam, *The Golden Legend*
    48 pp, perfectbound, $5.00
David Hilton, *Penguins*
    24 pp, hand-sewn, $3.00
Joanne Kyger, *Up My Coast*
    24 pp, hand-sewn, $3.00
Frank Stewart, *The Open Water*
    64 pp, perfectbound, $5.00
Arthur Sze, *Dazzled*
    60 pp, perfectbound, $5.00
John Brandi, *The Cowboy from Phantom Banks*
    80 pp, smythe-sewn, $6.95
Peter Wild, *The Light on Little Mormon Lake*
    32 pp, hand-sewn, $4.00
Kirk Robertson, *Two Weeks Off*
    48 pp, hand-sewn, $5.00
Norbert Krapf, *Circus Songs*
    32 pp, hand-sewn, $4.00
Cole Swensen, *It's Alive She Says*
    88 pp, smythe-sewn, $5.00
Joan Wolf, *The Divided Sphere*
    96 pp, smythe-sewn, $5.00
Michael Conway, *The Odyssey Singer*
    88 pp, smythe-sewn, $5.00
Eugene Lesser, *Drug Abuse in Marin County*
    136 pp, smythe-sewn, $8.95
Adele Langendorf, *Denial*
    64 pp, smythe-sewn, $5.00
William Witherup, *Collected Poems*
    224 pp, smythe-sewn, $10.00
Frank Stewart, *Flying the Red Eye*
    56 pp, smythe-sewn, $8.00

Floating Island I
    120 pp, smythe-sewn, $6.95
Floating Island II
    184 pp, perfectbound, $8.95
Floating Island III
    160 pp, perfectbound, $12.95